Schaum
Making Music Me[barcode]

By John W. Schaum

Level Four

T0081996

FOREWORD

This edition incorporates numerous refinements compiled by a team of piano teaching experts based on the evaluation of extensive use in actual teaching situations. The result is a volume that combines the proven merit and usefulness of the original edition with added benefits for students and ease of use for teachers.

Level Four presents harmonic minor scales with pieces in many minor keys, polyphonic music, three-staff reading, 2/2, 3/2 and 12/8 time signatures, parallel major and minor, theme and variations, medley form, and white key sharps. Wrist staccato and cross hand playing are explored. Built-in educational aids include key signature flash cards and rhythmic preparatory drills.

Music styles range from Bach to Beethoven, Handel to Chopin, and Dvorak to jazz. American composers include John Philip Sousa, Edward MacDowell, Victor Herbert and Mrs. H.H.A. Beach.

Self-help is encouraged by the Reference Pages (front and rear inside covers) and the Music Dictionary (page 46). The student can sound out pronunciations of musical terms by using the phonetic syllables provided.

The Schaum *Making Music Method* consists of **six books**, from Primer Level through Level 5

Schaum Publications, Inc.
10235 N. Port Washington Rd. • Mequon, WI 53092
www.schaumpiano.net

© Copyright 1964 and 1985 by Schaum Publications, Inc., Mequon, Wisconsin
International Copyright Secured • All Rights Reserved • Printed in U.S.A.
ISBN-13: 978-1-62906-028-6

CONTENTS

To the Teacher:

Student musicianship is developed by a well-balanced curriculum that teaches note reading, finger strength and dexterity, music theory, and music appreciation. It is recommended that one theory book, one technic book and several repertoire selections be used to supplement this method book. Choices may be found at our web site at *www.schaumpiano.net*.

Finger workouts and rhythm clapping should be used as presented. Key signature flash card drills (page 3) should be used frequently. Repetition helps make a lasting impression.

Review work and memorizing should be regular part of the student's assignments. As the pupil advances through the book, there will be pieces that are especially well-liked. These are good choices for memory work. An accumulation of memorized pieces becomes the student's repertoire.

Schaum's Curriculum for Musicianship Development

Student musicianship is developed by a balanced curriculum that includes:
- Note Reading and Music Theory
- Finger Strength and Dexterity
- Music Appreciation and Repertoire Development
- Rhythmic Training and Ensemble Experience

The Schaum website contains descriptions and complets contents of all our books and materials.

www.schaumpiano.net

SCHAUM FLASH CARDS

The following flash cards provide drill in key signature identification. They should be given to the pupil to study at home. The student brings the cards to every lesson until he can recognize every signature "in a flash" in two ways: major and relative minor. For each card, the pupil should recite the sharps or flats in correct order.

The following slogan will be helpful in remembering the order of the seven sharps: **F**ast **C**ars **G**o **D**angerously **A**round **E**very **B**end. A helpful memory aid in learning the flat succession is the word: **BEAD** followed by **G C F.** It should be pointed out that the seven sharps are in the exact opposite order of the seven flats.

To quickly identify the major sharp key signatures, go up a half step from the last sharp. For example in the signature of three sharps — the last sharp is G♯ — a half step above G♯ is A — therefore, the key name is A major. The major flat keys get their name from the second last flat. Take the signature of four flats — the second last flat is A♭ — therefore the key name is A♭ major. (Exception — Key of F which has one flat — B♭).

To determine any minor key signature, the key name is three scale degrees below the major key name. To illustrate, look at the signature of five sharps. The major key name is B — three scale degrees below B is G♯ — therefore the minor key name is G♯.

CAUTION: The signature on one of the flash cards is intentionally wrong. This will intensify the student's power of observation.

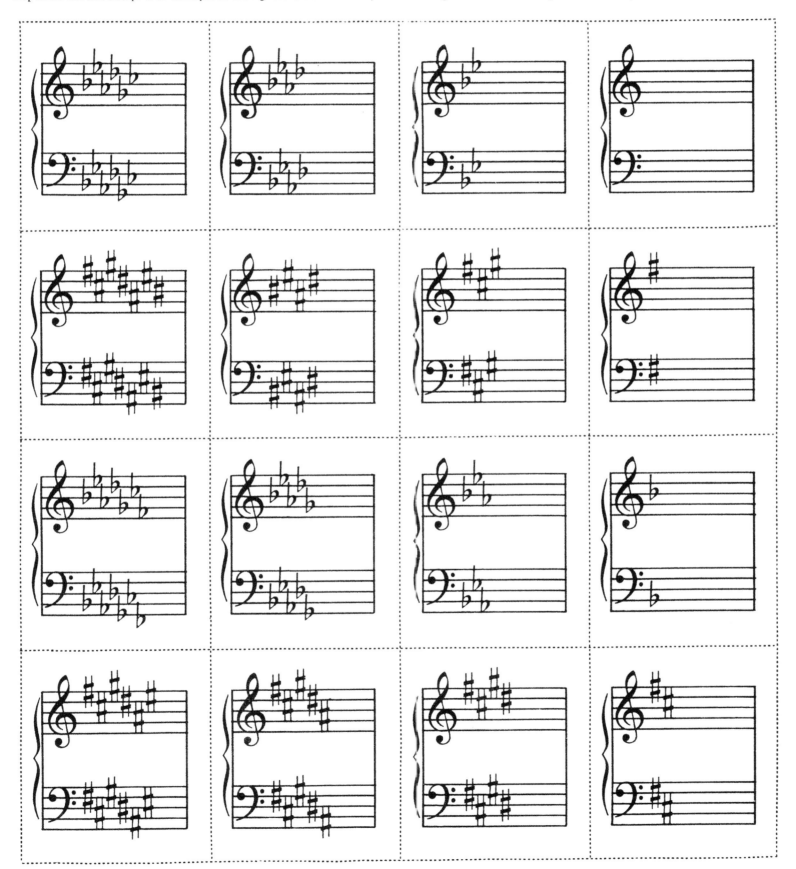

4

Key of C Major or A minor	Key of B♭ Major or G minor	Key of A♭ Major or F minor	Key of G♭ Major or E♭ minor
No sharps or flats	2 Flats: B♭, E♭	4 Flats: B♭, E♭, A♭, D♭	6 Flats: B♭, E♭, A♭, D♭ G♭, C♭

Key of G Major or E minor	Key of A Major or F♯ minor	This key signature is purposely not correct. The sharps are misplaced. This is to check for student allertness.	Key of C♯ Major or A♯ minor
1 Sharp: F♯	3 Sharps: F♯, C♯, G♯		7 Sharps: F♯, C♯, G♯, D♯ A♯, E♭ B♯

Key of F Major or D minor	Key of E♭ Major or C minor	Key of D♭ Major or B♭ minor	Key of C♭ Major or A♭ minor
1 Flats: B♭	3 Flats: B♭, E♭, A♭	5 Flats: B♭, E♭, A♭, D♭ G♭	7 Flats: B♭, E♭, A♭, D♭ G♭, C♭, F♭

Key of D Major or B minor	Key of E Major or C♯ minor	Key of B Major or G♯ minor	Key of F♯ Major or D♯ minor
2 Sharps: F♯, C♯	4 Sharps: F♯, C♯, G♯, D♯	5 Sharps: F♯, C♯, G♯, D♯ A♯	6 Sharps: F♯, C♯, G♯, D♯ A♯, E♯

Syncopated Windshield Wipers

(A Study in Jazz*)

Jazz is an American innovation in music characterized by lively syncopated rhythms. It has its roots in ragtime style.

Welcome to Level Four

In this book you will meet many new composers and get acquainted with their music. New styles of composition and interesting rhythms will add to your enjoyment. You will be introduced to the minor scales and learn many fascinating pieces in minor keys.

As you progress, you will encounter new techniques such as wrist staccato and arpeggio playing. You will get familiar with great classic writers as well as outstanding American composers. You will thoroughly enjoy "Making Music at the Piano."

Driftwood

(Arpeggio Waltz)

FINGER WORKOUT

Repeat 5 times daily

Teacher's Note: The above "Finger Workout" is an excellent preparatory for "Safety Cadets" since it combines the D-major tonality with the basic rhythm pattern of the piece (♩♫)

Safety Cadets

Animato M M ♩=108

Farmers' Market

Allegro M.M. ♪=160

* Beethoven

* Ludwig van Beethoven (BAY-toe-ven) 1770-1827, was a very famous composer born in Bonn, Germany, and is considered to be one of the greatest of all time. He is best known for his nine symphonies and 32 piano sonatas. He also wrote many pieces of chamber music (for small instrumental groups) and vocal music. This piece is based on a theme from his *Sonatina in G Major.*

Additional music of Beethoven is available in the album, *Best of Eeethoven,* and as sheet music solos, *Fur Elise,* and *Beethoven's Fifth Symphony* (1st Movement theme).

Davey Jones' Locker

(Three-Staff Reading)

H. W. Petrie*

* American song writer whose career flourished in the 1890's.

care, _____ _____ Sail-ors who brave the here-af - ter, Or your bones _____ Will go down to Da - vy Jones. _____

rit.

*8

* The number 8 followed by a dotted line is called an *octave lower sign.* The notes in the staff above are to be played one octave lower than written. This affects only the notes in the *bottom staff;* notes in the middle and upper staff are not changed.

Tulip Festival

Dart Game

(Wrist Staccato)

Teacher's Note: When playing the consecutive 6ths in the right hand, tell the student to "lock the hand" at the space between the thumb and 5th finger required to play the 6ths. The same idea can be used when playing consecutive 3rds.

14

Victor Herbert   John Philip Sousa

TWO GREAT AMERICAN COMPOSERS

Victor Herbert, although born in Ireland, spent the last 37 years of his life in the United States and established his fame as a composer and conductor here. Therefore, he is usually considered an *American* composer. He is best known for many songs from his 43 operettas. *In Old New York* is a theme from the operetta, *The Red Mill.*

John Philip Sousa is famous throughout the world as a composer of marches and is known as the "march king." He conducted his own band, performing in hundreds of cities, towns, fairs, and expositions all over the United States and in many foreign countries. A large brass instrument, called the *Sousaphone,* was designed for Sousa's Marine Band and is still commonly used today. *Stars and Stripes Forever* is Sousa's most famous march.

In Old New York

Allegretto M.M. ♩=112-120

Victor Herbert (1859-1924)

Stars and Stripes Forever

Con brio M.M. ♩ = 120-126

John Phillip Sousa (1854-1932)

Winter Carnival Waltz

A. Czibulka (1842-1894)
Arr. by John W. Schaum

Alphons Czibulka (chee BOOL kah) was a prolific Hungarian composer. At the age of twenty-three he became a choirmaster in Vienna. Later he served in the 17th regiment of the Hungarian infantry with which he made the campaign in Italy. Following this, he returned to Vienna as a bandmaster. In addition to his large number of piano compositions, he wrote three operettas and one opera. He was born May 14, 1842 and died October 27, 1894.

Minor Scale Story

Every major scale has a relative minor scale. All minor scales start on the sixth tone of the relative major. All minor key signatures are the same as the relative majors.

The most important minor scale is the HARMONIC minor. It consists of eight tones progressing in alphabetical order. The eight tones called DEGREES, have number names 1, 2, 3, 4, 5, 6, 7, 8. Half steps occur between 2 and 3, 5 and 6 and between 7 and 8. The distance between all the other degrees is a whole step. Exception — between 6 and 7 is always a step and a half.

A MINOR SCALE PATTERN
(Relative of C Major)

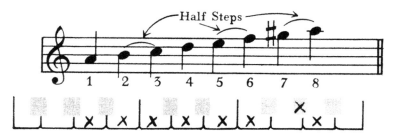

DIRECTIONS: In the following eight scales, add sharps or flats where necessary so that the half steps and whole steps occur in the proper places. Draw slurs between 2 and 3, 5 and 6, and between 7 and 8. Place check marks on the small keyboards.

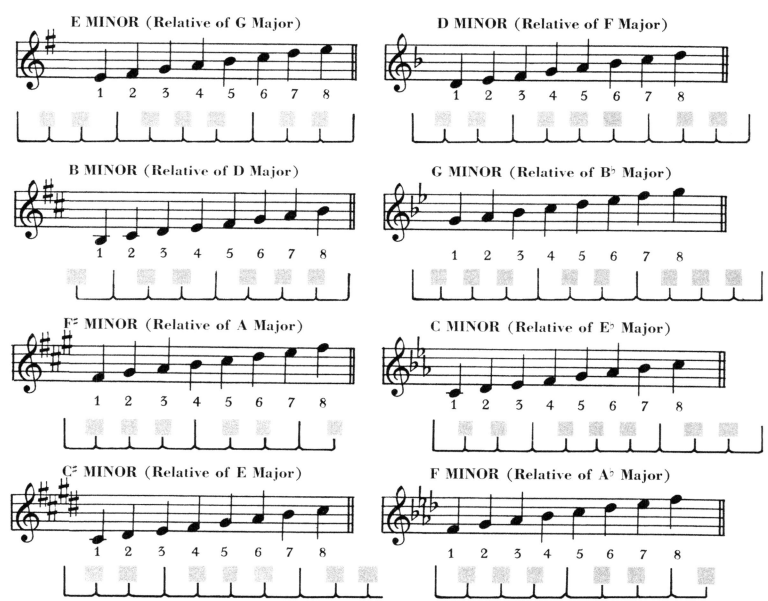

Note: After the sharps and flats have been properly inserted, play the scales on the piano.

FINGER WORKOUT

Scale of A minor (Harmonic Minor):

Repeat 5 times daily

Deserted Farm
(Key of A Minor)

Edward MacDowell, Op.51, No.8
(1861-1908)

Larghetto M.M. ♩ = 66-76

✱ Note: Tenuto *(tay NEW toe)* Held on, sustained. Abbreviation: *Ten.*

EDWARD MacDOWELL

One of America's great composers of classical music is Edward MacDowell. He was born December 18, 1861 in New York. His career was wide and varied. He concertized as a pianist and headed the first music department at Columbia University.

During this busy schedule he created many wonderful piano pieces, songs, symphonies, concertos and sonatas. The "Deserted Farm" is a theme from his famous "Woodland Sketches" suite. His life ended in New York on January 23, 1908.

FINGER WORKOUT

Slavonic Dance

(Key of E Minor)

* Anton Dvorak, Op. 72, No. 10
(1841-1904)

* Anton Dvorak (DVOR-zhock) was born in Czechoslovakia and was one of the most famous composers of that country. He wrote symphonies, chamber music, vocal music, and piano music. He was one of the few composers who wrote original music for *piano duet*. This piece is a theme transcribed from a duet. His compositions reflect the folk music and songs of his native country.

Dvorak visited the U.S. in 1892 and stayed for three years. During that time he composed his famous "New World Symphony."

FINGER WORKOUT

Scale of G minor (Harmonic Minor):

Repeat 5 times daily

Meadowlands March

(Key of G Minor)

Maestoso M.M. ♩=112

Traditional

This melody was a *theme of freedom* used by the people of European countries who fought valiantly to liberate their homelands during World War II.

FLASH CARD DRILLS: Review the flash cards (page 3) with special emphasis on reciting the *minor key* signature names.

Masks

DIRECTIONS: The following piece is to be played with *one hand alone;* one hand is to play the treble and bass parts simultaneously. First, play it entirely with the left hand; then, with the right hand. Notice how the *major key* sounds bright and happy, representing the mythological Greek god of comedy. The *minor key* sounds dark and sad, portraying the ancient god of tragedy.

Note: The key of G minor is the *parallel minor* of the key of G major. Although both scales start on the same tone, they have different key signatures.

Making Music Quiz No. 1

DIRECTIONS: Match each musical term at the left with the correct definition at the right by inserting the corresponding alphabetical letter on the proper dotted line. For example 1 means "heavy and firm", therefore the letter i has been placed on the dotted line.

Score 5 for each correct answer. A total score of 65 is passing, 70 is fair, 80 is good and 90 or above is excellent.

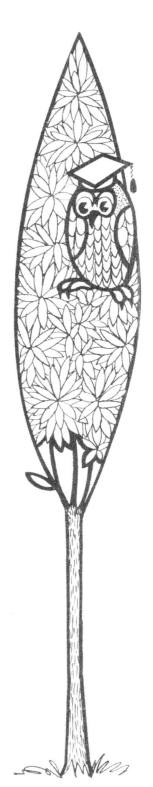

...i... 1.   pesante

.... 2.

.... 3.   jazz

.... 4.   Tempo di Valse

.... 5.   Beethoven

.... 6.   the sound of major

.... 7.   G major and E minor

.... 8.   Stars and Stripes Forever

.... 9.

.... 10.   ten.

.... 11.   *ppp*

.... 12.   Con moto

.... 13.   grazioso

.... 14.   the sound of minor

.... 15.   Victor Herbert

.... 16.   G major and G minor

.... 17.

.... 18.   Dvorak

.... 19.   Edward MacDowell

.... 20.

a. major key and its parallel minor

b. signature for F major or D minor

c. pianississimo (as soft as possible)

d. in a graceful style

e. signature for B♭ major or G minor

f. great American composer of light opera

g. with motion, not dragging

h. great Czech composer

i. heavy and firm

j. great German composer

k. signature for G major or E minor

l. great American classic composer

m. syncopated music of American origin

n. signature of D major or B minor

o. bright and happy

p. a composition by Sousa

q. tenuto (hold on, sustained)

r waltz time

s dark and gray

t. major key and its relative minor

Total Score ....

Four Seasons Suite

SPRING (Mendelssohn's Spring Song)
Allegro M.M. ♩=132

SUMMER (In the Good Old Summertime–Evans)
Allegro M.M. ♩=132

Note: Consult the Dictionary on page 46 for the meanings of the different terms used in "Four Season's Suite".

AUTUMN (Thanksgiving Hymn)
Andante M.M. ♩=96

WINTER (Jingle Bells - Pierpont)
Vivace M.M. ♩=160

Wayside Picnic Table

Mrs. H. H. A. Beach Op. 36, No. 3
(1867-1944)

Mrs. H. H. A. Beach was born in New Hampshire. She is regarded as one of America's outstanding women composers. Her works include piano solos, a symphony, a concerto, chamber music, songs and anthems.

Here's a supplementary album with more music by American women:

WOMEN COMPOSERS of the UNITED STATES

The Juggler

Allegro M.M. ♩=104

* Dussek (1760-1812)

White key sharp

* Jan Ladislav Dussek (DOO-sek) was a concert pianist, teacher, and composer born in Austria and well known in Russia, Lithuania, France, and England.

Two Types of Music
1. Monophonic

The word *monophonic* consists of two parts: *mono* and *phonic,* meaning "one sound." In music it describes a single melody with an accompaniment (also sometimes called *homophonic* music). Most musical compositions belong to this category. The tunes "Merrily We Roll Along" and "London Bridge" are examples of monophonic music.

"London Bridge" (of nursery-rhyme fame) has been moved to the United States! Because the 140-year old bridge needed repair and was no longer suitable for modern London's heavy traffic, it was sold for 2½ million dollars, taken apart (10,276 blocks of granite) and shipped (130,000 tons) to Lake Havasu City, Arizona where it took forty men working twenty-three months to re-assemble it!

2. Polyphonic

When two or more melodies are played at the same time, the effect is called *polyphonic* music. *Poly* means "many" and *phonic* means "sound;" therefore polyphonic means "many sounds." When the tunes "Merrily We Roll Along" and "London Bridge" are played simultaneously they become *polyphonic* music. The familiar musical *round*, "Frere Jacques," and the Pachelbel "Canon" are other examples of polyphonic music.

Northern Song

(Polyphonic Music)

Robert Schumann, Op. 68, No. 41
(1810-1856)

Robert Schumann was not only a great composer, but he also sponsored and encouraged the careers of other composers. Brahms was one of his proteges. The composition "Northern Song" is from Schumann's "Album for the Young." He subtitled it "A Greeting to Niels W. Gade" which was a tribute to the rising young Danish composer who was from the North. Notice how Schumann ingeniously spells out the name GADE several times in the piece.

King's Hunting Song

Niels W. Gade was born in Copenhagen, Denmark. He was the founder of the Scandinavian school of music. He was in great demand as an orchestral conductor throughout Europe. Although his compositions never achieved wide recognition, his influence was tremendous. Because of Gade, the great Edvard Grieg was able to develop the specific traits of Scandinavian folk music.

Desert Patrol

* Cesar Cui (1835-1918)

Allegro non tróppo M.M. ♩=126

SPECIAL ASSIGNMENT

"Desert Patrol" is in the key of G minor. Review the "Finger Workout" on page 21.

* Cesar Cui was a Russian composer, newspaper critic, and expert in military fortifications. This piece was transcribed from his opus 50, for violin and piano.

* The wavy line indicates a *rolled chord.* This means that the notes are to be played individually, in arpeggio style, rapidly moving from bottom to top with bass notes first, followed by treble notes. The notes are to be timed so that the top note in the treble is struck precisely on the beat of the written chord.

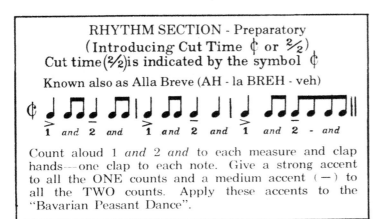

RHYTHM SECTION - Preparatory
(Introducing Cut Time ¢ or 2/2)
Cut time (2/2) is indicated by the symbol ¢

Known also as Alla Breve (AH - la BREH - veh)

Count aloud 1 *and* 2 *and* to each measure and clap hands—one clap to each note. Give a strong accent to all the ONE counts and a medium accent (—) to all the TWO counts. Apply these accents to the "Bavarian Peasant Dance".

Johann Sebastian Bach is considered by most authorities as one of the greatest musicians of all time. Although he is best known for his polyphonic music, he was also a master of melody.

Additional music of Bach is available in the album, *Best of Bach* and in sheet music solos, *Joy Prelude* and *Minuet Medley*.

Bavarian Peasant Dance

(Polyphonic Music)

Note: The sustained bass note is called a DRONE BASS. It represents the bagpipe (also known as a musette) which was played at folk dances in Bach's day.

J. S. Bach (1685–1750)

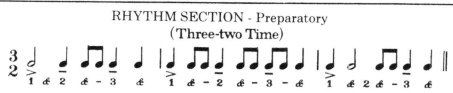

RHYTHM SECTION - Preparatory
(Three-two Time)

In ¾ time, there are three counts per measure and a half note gets one count. Accent the first count prominently and give the second and third counts a slight emphasis. Count aloud 1 & 2 & 3 & to each measure and clap hands– one clap to each note. This is the rhythm pattern for "Hornpipe".

Handel and Bach were both born in Germany in the same year, 1685. Although they lived in towns only eighty miles apart, these great masters never met. Handel moved to England where he spent the major part of his life. He became a British citizen, and was honored by burial in Westminster Abbey, a church where English royalty are entombed.

Hornpipe
(Polyphonic Music)

Allegro M.M. ♩= 58-63   George Frederick Handel (1685-1759)

Birthday Bouquet

(Theme and Variations)

Theme (By Mildred Hill)

Moderato M.M. ♩=112

Variation I (Boogie)

Animato M.M. ♩=116

Variation II (Ragtime)

Allegro M.M. ♩=138

Variation III (Blues)
Larghetto M.M. ♩=88

Variation IV (Jazz)
Giocoso M.M. ♩=116

FINGER WORKOUT

Scale of G-flat Major:

Repeat 5 times daily

Black Key Mazurka

This piece will often require placing the thumb on a black key. Although it is preferable to use the thumb on white keys, this cannot be done here because of the key signature. Other key signatures with four or more sharps or flats may also require the thumb on a black key.

Key of G♭ Major, Six flats (Flat every note except F)

A. Herzog*

Vivace M.M. ♩=112-120

*A. Herzog — Viennese composer of light music. Career flourished in early 1900's.

Day Dreaming

RHYTHM SECTION - Preparatory
(Introducing 12/8 Time)

Count aloud 1-2-3-4-5-6-7-8-9-10-11-12 to each measure and clap hands-one clap to each note. Give a strong accent (>) to all the ONE and SEVEN counts and a medium accent (–) to all the FOUR and TEN counts. Apply these accents to "Day Dreaming".

In this piece, each metronome "click" equals a *dotted quarter note.* In 12/8 time, it is often easier to think of *four main counts* in each measure (one for each metronome click) instead of attempting to count all twelve numbers.

SPECIAL ASSIGNMENT
As a preparatory, play "Whispering Winds" in blocked chord style, as shown below.

etc.

PHRASING

The sign of the slur which is used in music has different meanings. It is frequently used to connect a group of notes which can be played in one hand-position. For example, notice the right hand clusters which occur throughout the piece "Whispering Winds." The slur is also used to join a series of notes which make up a phrase. This is illustrated by the slurs employed in the left hand in this piece. It is not always necessary to lift the hand or release the pedal at the end of each slur. Occasionally, this procedure is acceptable. There is no rigid rule on when to release or when not to release at the end of a slur. This is determined solely on how each piece is interpreted.

Whispering Winds

F. Braungardt, Op. 6
(See bottom of page 41)

F. Braungardt (BROWN-gart) German composer of the late 19th Century.

FINGER WORKOUT

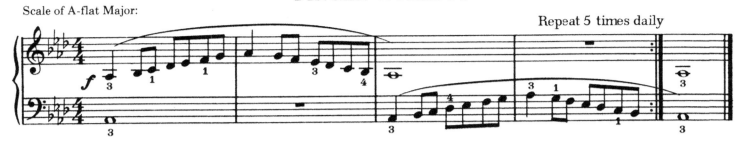

Scale of A-flat Major:

Repeat 5 times daily

Town Crier

(Key of A-flat major)

Allegro M.M. ♩ = 152-168

Traditional

FINGER WORKOUT

Scale of F minor (Harmonic Minor):

Repeat 5 times daily

Dusk

Allegretto M.M. ♩=112   (Key of F minor)   * Chopin, Op. 70, No. 2 (1810-1849)

Note: The piece "Town Crier" on page 42 is in the key of A♭ major and "Dusk" is in the key of F minor (relative to A♭ major).

* Frederic Chopin (SHOW-pan) is often called the "poet of the keyboard" because he was one of the greatest composers for the piano. He was born in a small village near Warsaw, Poland, and was active as a composer, pianist, and teacher. This piece is transcribed from one of his "Nocturnes."

Scattered Showers

Making Music Quiz No. 2

DIRECTIONS: Match each musical sign at the left with the correct definition at the right by inserting the corresponding alphabetical letter on the proper dotted line.

Score 5 for each correct answer. A total score of 65 is passing, 70 is fair, 80 is good and 90 or above is excellent.

.... 1. Con brio

.... 2.

.... 3. monophonic

.... 4. musette

.... 5. scherzando

.... 6. ragtime

.... 7. 𝄪

.... 8. |♩ ♩♩ ♩|

.... 9. Handel

.... 10. polyphonic

.... 11.

.... 12. boogie

.... 13. |♫♪ ♫♪ ♫♪ ♫♪|

.... 14. ¢

.... 15. Schumann

.... 16. blues

.... 17. Mrs. H.H.A. Beach

.... 18.

.... 19. Niels Gade

.... 20. drone bass

---

a. a measure in 3/2 time

b. British (German born) composer

c. rhythmic folk music with a mood of depression

d. music with two or more melodies sounding at once

e. famous U.S. woman composer

f. cut time (2/2)

g. with life and spirit

h. signature of A♭ major or F minor

i. a bagpipe

j. early American syncopated music, forerunner of jazz

k. playful and merry

l. double sharp

m. the founder of Scandinavian music

n. music with a single melody

o. white key sharp

p. a measure in 12/8 time

q. a deep sustained tone

r. signature of G♭ major or E♭ minor

s. a rhythmic type of polyphonic music

t. German master composer

Total Score ....

MUSIC DICTIONARY

Terms listed here are limited to those commonly found in Level Four methods and supplements, however many elementary terms such as *forte* and *piano* are not included because of limited space. The accented syllable is shown in *capital* letters. Tempo marks which consist of two or three words, such as *Allegro con brio*, or *poco piu moto* are not listed here. It is intended that such terms be looked up one word at a time. This gives the pupil experience that will be valuable when working with a larger dictionary.

accel. = accelerando (ahk-sell-er-ON-doh) Becoming gradually faster in speed.

adagio (ah-DAH-jee-oh) Slow; slowly.

alla breve (ah-lah-BREV) Time signature equivalent to 2/2, also known as *cut time* (half note gets one count). Indicated by the symbol: ¢

allegretto (ah-leh-GRET-toh) A little slower than *allegro*.

allegro (ah-LEG-grow) Fast, quickly.

andante (ahn-DAHN-tay) Moderately slow.

andantino (ahn-dahn-TEE-noh) A little faster than *andante*.

anima (AH-nee-mah) Spirit, life, animation.

animato (ah-nee-MAH-toh) Lively, spirited.

arpeggio (are-PED-jee-oh) Rapidly playing the notes of a chord one at a time, consecutively, either upward or downward.

a tempo (ah TEHM-poh) Return to the previous tempo.

blues Slow wistful style of music with jazz-type rhythms originating with American Blacks during the early 1900's.

boogie woogie (BOO-gee WOO-gee) Type of blues music with tempo ranging from slow to fast; usually played on the piano with an ostinato bass accompaniment pattern and improvised-style syncopated melody.

brillante (bree-LAHN-teh) Brilliant, showy.

brio (BREE-oh) Vigor, spirit, gusto.

cantabile (cahn-TAH-bil-lay) Singing style.

chamber music Music involving a small group of performers for a small hall or parlor. Usually for various instrumental combinations from two to ten players. A common example is the string quartet.

con (KONE) With.

cut time Another name for *alla breve*.

degree Number given to each note of a major or minor scale in ascending sequence.

dolce (DOL-chay) Sweetly, softly.

doloroso (doh-loh-ROH-soh) Sadly, sorrowfully.

drone 1) Largest and lowest-sounding pipe of a bagpipe. 2) Long sustained note, usually in the bass.

espressivo (ehs-preh-SEE-voh) With expression and emotion.

giocoso (jee-oh-KOH-soh) Humorously, playfully.

grazioso (gra-tsee-OH-soh) Gracefully.

harmonic minor See page 18.

homophonic See page 28.

hornpipe Lively English folk dance for one person, at one time popular with sailors.

jazz Style of American popular music evolving from ragtime, usually with many syncopations, an improvised style, and prominent beat. Often jazz music is completely improvised.

larghetto (lahr-GET-oh) Tempo a little faster than *largo*.

largo (LAHR-goh) Very slow, solemn.

legato (lah-GAH-toh) Notes played in a smooth and connected manner. Usually indicated with a *slur*.

leggiero (led-jee-AIR-oh) Light, delicate. Abbreviation: *legg*.

maestoso (my-ess-TOH-soh) Majestic, dignified; proudly.

marcato (mahr-CAH-toh) Marked, emphasized.

mazurka (mah-ZUR-kah) Polish folk dance in triple meter. Tempo ranges from lively to slow, depending upon the style.

metronome (MET-roh-nome) Device to determine tempo or speed in music. Measured in beats per minute. The original mechanical metronome was invented by J.N. Maelzel, therefore the abbreviation, M.M. (Maelzel's metronome).

mf = mezzo forte (MET-zoh FOHR-tay) Medium loud; softer than *forte*.

minor Chord, melody, or scale often having a sad, mysterious, or spooky sound.

misterioso (miss-teer-ee-OH-soh) Mysteriously.

M.M. = Maelzel's metronome.

moderato (mah-dur-AH-toh) At a moderate speed.

molto (MOHL-toh) Very, much.

monophonic See page 28.

moto (MOH-toh) Motion, movement.

mp = mezzo piano (MET-zoh pee-YAA-noh) Medium soft; louder than *piano*.

musette (mew-ZETT) Instrument like a bagpipe, used in folk dances of Bach's time.

non troppo (NOHN TROHP-poh) Not too much.

op. = opus (OH-puss) Musical work; may be a composition of any length from a short single piece to a full symphony. Usually numbered in chronological order.

opera (AH-per-ah) Secular musical drama with vocal solos, ensembles, and choruses with orchestral accompaniment. Often includes dancing and ballet sequences. Staged with a full array of costumes, props, scenery, lighting, special effects, etc.

operetta (ah-per-ETT-ah) Short *opera*, usually not serious in plot and with some spoken dialogue.

ostinato (ahs-tin-NAH-toh) Melodic phrase 4 to 8 measures long which is repeated over and over (usually at the same pitch) while other parts are involved in different variations, often in contrapuntal style. An ostinato is commonly used in boogie and rock music.

parallel minor Minor tonality or scale having the same starting note as a major scale, but a different key signature. See page 22.

pastorale (pahs-toh-RAH-leh) Peaceful, calm, unhurried mood characteristic of a shepherd or rural area.

pesante (peh-SAHN-teh) Heavy, weighty.

piu (PEE-oo) More.

Continued on Back Inside Cover

Certificate
of Progress

This certifies that

_____

has successfully completed

LEVEL FOUR

of the Schaum

Making Music Method

and is eligible for advancement to
LEVEL FIVE

_____
Teacher

_____
Date